The California
Gold Rush

Sabrina Crewe and Michael V. Uschan

Gareth Stevens Publishing

A WORLD ALMANAC EDUCATION GROUP COMPANY

To Barbara Roark, librarian extraordinaire

Please visit our web site at: www.garethstevens.com
For a free color catalog describing Gareth Stevens Publishing's list of high-quality books and multimedia programs, call 1-800-542-2595 (USA) or 1-800-387-3178 (Canada). Gareth Stevens Publishing's fax: (414) 332-3567.

Library of Congress Cataloging-in-Publication Data

Crewe, Sabrina.
    The California Gold Rush / by Sabrina Crewe and Michael V. Uschan.
      p. cm. — (Events that shaped America)
    Includes bibliographical references and index.
    ISBN 0-8368-3393-7 (lib. bdg.)
    1. California—Gold discoveries—Juvenile literature. 2. California—History—1846-1850—Juvenile literature. 3. Frontier and pioneer life—California—Juvenile literature. [1. California—Gold discoveries. 2. California—History—1846-1850. 3. Frontier and pioneer life—California.] I. Uschan, Michael V., 1948- . II. Title. III. Series.
    F865.C895   2003
    979.4'04—dc21
                                                2002030994

First published in 2003 by
Gareth Stevens Publishing
A World Almanac Education Group Company
330 West Olive Street, Suite 100
Milwaukee, WI 53212 USA

Copyright © 2003 by Gareth Stevens Publishing.

Produced by Discovery Books
Editor: Sabrina Crewe
Designer and page production: Sabine Beaupré
Photo researcher: Sabrina Crewe
Maps and diagrams: Stefan Chabluk
Gareth Stevens editorial direction: Mark J. Sachner
Gareth Stevens art direction: Tammy Gruenewald
Gareth Stevens production: Jessica Yanke

Photo credits: Bancroft Library, University of California: p. 12; California History Room, California State Library: p. 16; Corbis: pp. 4, 5, 11, 13, 14, 17, 18, 21, 25, 26, 27; Little Bighorn Battlefield National Monument: p. 24; North Wind Picture Archives: cover, pp. 6, 7, 9, 10, 15, 19, 20, 22, 23.

Printed in the United States of America

1 2 3 4 5 6 7 8 9 07 06 05 04 03

Contents

Introduction

This cartoon from the Gold Rush period shows gold hunters rushing off to California. Newspaper and magazine cartoons made fun of people with gold fever.

Gold Fever

Throughout history, people have often wanted to own gold. This greed for gold, sometimes known as "gold fever," spread quickly and made people act in a rather crazy way. Many years ago, gold fever caused something important to happen when gold was discovered in California.

Discovery in California

Before 1848, hardly any Americans lived in California. It wasn't even part of the United States. But when gold was found there in 1848, everything changed. In just four years, almost 250,000 people, mostly white Americans, arrived to settle in California. The period when people flocked to California to search for gold is known as the California Gold Rush.

Westward Expansion

The Gold Rush in California lasted until about 1856. Then it moved on to other areas of the West, such as Nevada, Utah, and Colorado. Those areas were also soon settled by Americans who came west from states in the East. This **migration** of Americans is called westward **expansion**. It is how white settlers came to inhabit large areas that, before the Gold Rush, had been Native American homelands.

An Attack of Gold Fever

"I looked on for a moment; a frenzy seized my soul; . . . piles of gold rose up before me at every step; castles of marble, dazzling the eye with their rich appliances; thousands of slaves, bowing to my beck and call; were among the fancies of my fevered imagination. In short, I had a very violent attack of the Gold Fever."

James H. Carson of Monterey, California, recalling how he felt when he saw a sack of gold nuggets, 1848

The Value of Gold

Gold is valuable partly because it is rare. It is also beautiful to look at and easy to work with. Gold can be hammered into slivers thinner than paper or shaped into jewelry and coins. It is brilliantly shiny and doesn't get rusty as some metals do. Gold has often been used as a unit of **currency** and as a measure of the value of other things.

Chapter One

California Under Many Flags

This Native hunter is from the Sierra Nevada region where gold was discovered in 1848.

Native Californians

Long before the Gold Rush brought Americans to California—for thousands of years, in fact—the area was home to Native Americans. There were probably about 300,000 people living there in more than 100 groups. They survived by hunting and gathering food. Some lived in **fertile** regions close to the Pacific Ocean and its good supply of seafood. Others lived in desert or mountain regions where food supplies were scarce.

The Spanish Empire

South of California, in the 1500s, Spain took over great areas of Central and South America, claiming them as part of the Spanish **Empire**. Spanish rulers saw the Native people and **natural resources** of the Americas as a source of wealth for them. They sent people to start **colonies** and force the Native people into slavery. With a huge Native workforce, Spain was able to exploit the colonies for its own gain. In the process, millions of Native people died of diseases brought from Europe or were killed by Spanish colonists.

The Spanish Empire moved into California in 1769 when a Catholic priest, Junípero Serra, arrived with a group of soldiers. Serra established a string of twenty-one **missions** that became centers for farming and ranching. Many Native Americans fled the newcomers, but thousands were forced by the soldiers into slave labor at the missions.

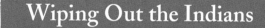

Wiping Out the Indians

Europeans—and their diseases—killed off most of the Native people of California. By the 1840s, after about eighty years of colonial rule, a population that had flourished for thousands of years was cut in half. By 1900, after thousands of settlers had arrived during the migration that was started by the Gold Rush, fewer than sixteen thousand Native Americans lived in California.

Spanish and Mexican settlers in California built first missions and then large ranches. This is a Californian ranch during the 1800s, before the arrival of Americans.

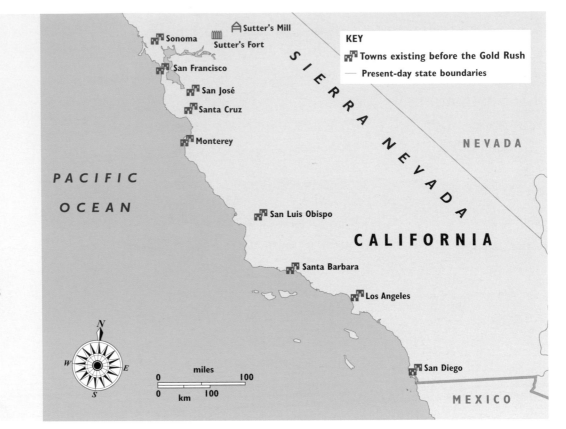

There were very few towns in California before the Gold Rush. This map shows where those towns were. It also shows Sutter's Mill, where the gold was discovered.

Mexico and the United States

In 1821, people living in Mexico revolted against their Spanish rulers. They won their freedom and established the **Republic** of Mexico, which included California. For the next twenty-five years, California was a Mexican **province** instead of a Spanish colony.

Across the continent, however, another nation had its eye on California. Most Americans still lived in the original thirteen states along the east coast, but settlers were spreading west. Many Americans believed that it was the destiny of the United States to rule the entire continent from the Atlantic to the Pacific Ocean.

In 1845, the United States offered to buy California from Mexico, but Mexico refused to sell. The two nations were already arguing about Texas, which had been Mexican and was now American. Things were getting hostile, and the Mexican War broke out in 1846.

The United States Acquires California

At that time, about two thousand American settlers were living in California under Mexican rule. On June 10, 1846—after they had heard about the Mexican War—a band of about thirty Americans raised their own flag and declared they were founding the California Republic. The Bear Flag Revolt, as it was called, did not last long. On July 9, 1846, the U.S. Navy arrived and claimed California as American.

The Mexican War officially ended in 1848 after both Mexico and the United States approved the **Treaty** of Guadalupe Hidalgo, signed on February 2. The treaty gave the United States more than 525,000 square miles (1,360,000 square kilometers) of land. This included what are now Utah, California, and Nevada and parts of Arizona, New Mexico, Colorado, and Wyoming. In 1850, California became a state.

The Bear Flag Revolt got its name from the image of a bear on the rebels' flag. That bear is still part of the California flag today.

Chapter Two

The Discovery at Sutter's Mill

Sutter named New Helvetia after Helvetia, or Switzerland, where he once lived. Today, the site is Sacramento, capital of California.

Sutter's Mill

One of the earliest settlers to arrive in California from the United States was Johann Augustus Sutter. In 1839, he got a land grant from the Mexican government and founded New Helvetia, known locally as Sutter's Fort. It became a center for trading and settlement at the junction of the American River and the Sacramento River.

In August 1847, Sutter and James Marshall, a carpenter, got together to build a **sawmill**. Sutter's Mill, as it was called, was 45 miles (72 kilometers) northeast of Sutter's Fort in the small mountain valley of Coloma.

This is a replica of the sawmill built by Marshall's men in Coloma. The replica stands on the site of the original mill, in what is now Marshall Gold Discovery Historic Park.

On the morning of January 24, 1848, Marshall was inspecting the new mill. Noticing something shiny in the river, Marshall picked up a gold-colored pebble. "Hey, boys," said Marshall to his workers, "by God, I believe I have found a gold mine."

Marshall showed Sutter what he had found. Sutter realized the gold could make him rich. He did not own the land the mill was on, but **leased** it—in exchange for clothing and food—from the Yalesummi people who lived there. In spite of this, Sutter thought the rights to the gold would be his.

Sutter's Dream

Sutter's dream of becoming rich turned into a nightmare. When word of the **strike** spread, gold seekers flooded onto Sutter's land, trampled over his fields, and damaged his buildings. Sutter failed to become rich by finding gold himself. He said, "By this sudden discovery of the gold, all my great plans were destroyed." Sutter was so bitter that in 1865 he left California for Pennsylvania.

Something Shining

"It was a clear cold morning; I shall never forget that morning. As I was taking my usual walk [by the mill] my eye was caught by a glimpse of something shining. . . . I reached my hand down and picked it up; it made my heart thump, for I felt certain it was gold. The piece was about half the size and of the shape of a pea."

James W. Marshall

This cartoon shows a hopeful gold hunter weighed down with all kinds of goods including a cooking pot on his head.

Gold Mine Found

"GOLD MINE FOUND—In the newly made raceway of the saw-mill recently erected by Captain Sutter, on the American [River], gold has been found in considerable quantities. . . . California, no doubt, is rich in mineral wealth."

The Californian *newspaper, with the first story about the gold discovery, San Francisco, March 15, 1848*

The News Gets Out

By mid-March 1848, news of the discovery had spread throughout California. Most Californians were not very excited, however, because small amounts of gold had been found before.

This attitude soon changed because of Sam Brannan, a San Francisco businessman. He bought shovels, picks, metal pans, and other things people needed to hunt gold. He then opened a store at Coloma. In early May, Brannan ran down the streets of San Francisco shouting loudly, "Gold! Gold! Gold from the American River!" Many people jumped on horses and headed for Sutter's Mill.

The Gold Rush Picks Up Speed

San Francisco and other California towns became deserted overnight. Farmers, storekeepers, and even doctors and ministers joined the mad dash for gold. Peaceful, beautiful

Coloma Valley became crowded with gold seekers. The hunt for riches soon spread north and south of the valley. Miners found gold everywhere.

By the end of 1848, between eight and ten thousand people were looking for gold, still quite a small number. That soon changed. California's military governor, Colonel Richard Mason, sent a report to the U.S. government about the gold. The news began to spread, first in the United States and then around the world.

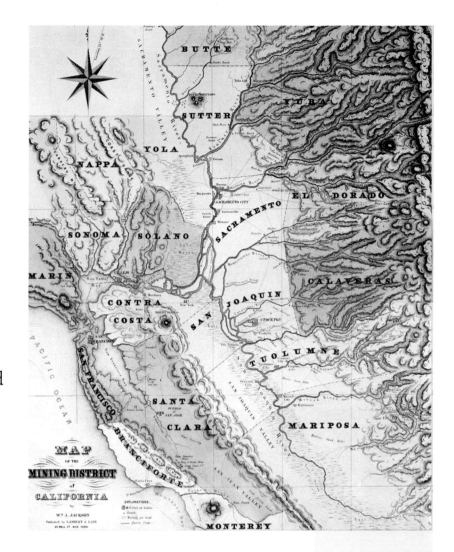

This map of California's gold mining region was drawn in 1851.

Vast Deposits

"The discovery of these vast **deposits** of gold has entirely changed the character of Upper California. Its people, before engaged in cultivating their small parcels of ground and guarding their herds of cattle and horses, have all gone to the mines, or are on their way thither; laborers of every trade have left their work benches, and tradesmen their shops; sailors desert their ships as fast as they arrive on the coast."

Colonel Richard B. Mason, military governor of California, in a report sent to Washington, D.C., August 17, 1848

Chapter Three

The Forty-Niners

AN ACCOUNT OF

CALIFORNIA,

AND THE

WONDERFUL GOLD REGIONS.

A New Arrival at the Gold Diggings.

WITH A DESCRIPTION OF

The Different Routes to California;

Information about the Country, and the Ancient and Modern Discoveries of Gold;

How to Test Precious Metals; Accounts of Gold Hunters;

TOGETHER WITH MUCH OTHER

Useful Reading for those going to California, or having Friends there.

ILLUSTRATED WITH MAPS AND ENGRAVINGS.

BOSTON:
PUBLISHED BY J. B. HALL, 66 CORNHILL.
For Sale at Skinner's Publication Rooms, 60½ Cornhill.

Price, 12½ cents.

This guide for travelers to California shows the most common method of traveling west. Americans had no idea what to expect when they set off to California, and so guides like this were useful.

The President Spreads the Word

On December 5, 1848, President James K. Polk confirmed the presence of gold in California. Polk's words made front page headlines in newspapers across North America and other continents. Gold fever became a raging epidemic that quickly spread worldwide.

The Forty-Niners

In 1849, about ninety thousand newcomers arrived in California. Gold seekers became known as "forty-niners." It is hard to believe today that so many people would leave their jobs to look for gold. But for most forty-niners, the reason was simple: it was a chance to have a better life.

Clementine

"In a cavern, in a canyon,
Excavating for a mine,
Lived a miner, forty-niner,
and his daughter Clementine."

Lyrics to "Clementine," a song of the Gold Rush era

How They Got There

Before 1849, most Americans could not have found California on a map. It was a long way from the United States, and no railroads connected the two halves of the continent. Over the next few years, thousands would die trying to make the journey west.

Most gold seekers chose to walk or ride a horse or wagon. To get to California, they had to cross the Great Plains, a large stretch of territory inhabited by Native Americans. This route took six months.

Other forty-niners traveled by sea. It took ships almost half a year to sail around the tip of South America to California from the eastern United States. Conditions on board the ships were terrible and crowded.

Some forty-niners sailed to Panama in Central America. From there, they traveled overland through dense, dangerous jungle to catch a second ship that carried them to California. This journey was shorter but more expensive.

Hopeful gold seekers find fresh air on the deck of a ship bound for California. Down below were dark, crowded sleeping quarters.

In the 1840s, most Americans had never seen an elephant. "Seeing the elephant" became a boast for anyone who had seen unusual things. The forty-niners who made their way to California had so many adventures and saw so many strange sights that they could proudly claim to have "seen the elephant."

The two African American miners in this 1852 photograph may have been working to buy their freedom from slavery.

The Miners

In 1848, more than half the workers in the gold fields were Indian slaves forced to labor for others. Some Indians mined gold on their own. However, because Native Americans had few rights and white people thought of them as inferior, many were robbed or cheated out of the gold they found.

In the first three years of the Gold Rush, California's African American population grew to more than two thousand people. Most African American miners were free men. Although some were brought to California as slaves, many were able to buy their freedom with gold they mined.

From All Over the World

Most forty-niners, about 80 percent, came from the United States. But thousands came farther, from countries in Europe and Asia. One of the largest groups of miners came from China. It was the first time large numbers of

Asians had come to North America. The Chinese **immigrants** worked hard, but they were discriminated against by whites for many decades.

Women Forty-Niners

The California Gold Rush was almost entirely male. The few women who came, however, found they could make money providing services to male forty-niners. They cooked, did laundry, and ran many small businesses.

One woman, Margaret Frink, made a large fortune by cooking. She wrote, "I have made about $18,000 ($360,000 today) worth of pies—about one-third of this has been clear profit."

By the end of the 1800s, a large Chinese community had grown up in San Francisco. This is a family in San Francisco's Chinatown in 1904.

Then and Now

The sums of money received and spent during the Gold Rush seem very low today. During the Gold Rush era, however, most workers earned only a few hundred dollars each year, so something that cost only $10 in 1848 was expensive. One way to understand the value of money then is to compare what something cost in the past to what it costs today. A general rule of thumb is that an item bought for $1 in 1848 would cost $20 today, or 20 times as much. A different rule applies to the value of gold, which is 25 times what it was then.

A Mineress

"I have become a mineress; that is, if having washed a pan of dirt with my own hands, and procured therefrom three dollars and twenty-five cents in gold dust . . . will entitle me to the name. . . . I wet my feet, tore my dress, spoilt a pair of new gloves, nearly froze my fingers, got an awful headache, took cold and lost a valuable breastpin. . . ."

Louisa Clapp, a doctor's wife in California, in a letter to her sister in the East

17

The Gold Rush Years

During the Gold Rush, there were so many people arriving that it was hard to find places to stay. The owner of this sheep pen made money using it as a hotel.

California's Rapid Growth

In 1848, California was home to about 150,000 Native Americans and 14,000 people of European and Mexican descent, including about 2,000 Americans. When gold was discovered, however, California's population boomed. By the end of 1860, it had grown to 380,000.

By 1849, Sacramento had grown up around Sutter's Fort and had 12,000 residents. The most amazing transformation came in San Francisco, where the wealth of the gold fields turned it into one of the world's major cities. In 1847, San Francisco had only 450 residents, and in mid-1848, it became deserted as its residents rushed to Sutter's Mill. By 1849, however, it had a population of over 20,000 people.

Miners set up tents outside of the central mining camps, close to where they were hunting for gold.

Mining Camps Appear

Hundreds of camps and makeshift towns sprang up around sites where gold was found. They had strange, colorful names, such as Poker Flat, Devil's Retreat, Mad Mule Gulch, Gouge Eye, and Poverty Hill. In the mining camps, businessmen and women set up stores, saloons, laundries, restaurants, and hotels. Often these businesses were run in tents or wooden shacks.

Miners living around the camps came to buy supplies and relax from their work. Their main entertainment was drinking and gambling. Mining camps were places where criminals could do well. Professional gamblers, con artists, and thieves filled the camps, intent on cheating forty-niners out of their gold.

Rascals with Soft Hands

"Hordes of pickpockets, robbers, thieves, and swindlers were mixed with men who had come with honest intentions. These rascals had lived all their lives by the sleight of hand and it was evident that they had not come to California with gold rings on their white, soft hands for the purpose of wielding the pick and pan in obtaining their wishes. Murders, theft and heavy robberies soon became the order of the day."

Forty-niner J. H. Carson

Gold mining underground was dangerous work. Miners were employed to spend long days in the dark tunnels, chipping gold deposits out of the rock.

Digging Deeper

After the first few years, the thousands of hopeful miners had exhausted gold deposits above ground. After that, the only way to strike gold was to dig underground to reach deposits buried deep in the rock. This meant drilling and digging deep **shafts**. Shaft mining was expensive, and only companies or people with large amounts of money could mine gold this way. Many forty-niners left California disheartened and penniless.

High Prices

Mining, however, was not the only way to become rich during the Gold Rush. Businessmen like Sam Brannan were able to sell supplies to miners at very high prices because the goods they sold were the only ones available. Brannan, for instance, bought iron pans for 20 cents ($4 today) and sold them at mining camps for $8 to $16 ($160 to $320).

In the early days of the Gold Rush, a loaf of bread that would cost 5 cents ($1 today) in New York sold for 75 cents ($15) in San Francisco. Other high prices included 50 cents ($10) for an egg and $40 ($800) for a blanket!

Other Ways to Make Money

There were many other ways to earn a living during the Gold Rush years. People worked as teamsters driving wagons to get supplies to miners. Doctors and dentists cared for people in the mining camps. Blacksmiths shod horses and mules and repaired mining equipment. People from every profession imaginable, including singers and actors, were able to move to California and charge high prices for their work.

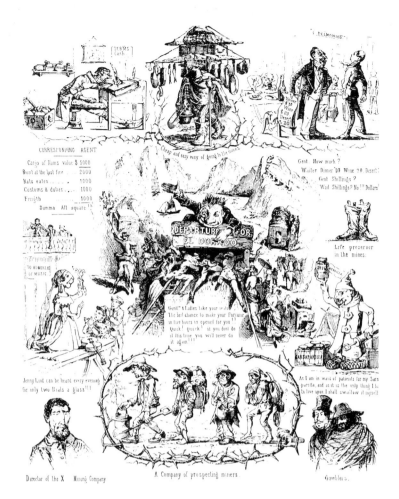

This cartoon ridicules the people in California during the Gold Rush. It shows those who cheated or made use of the forty-niners in a variety of ways.

The People Who Lost in the Gold Rush

Although many grew rich during the Gold Rush, the people who had lived in California the longest did not. The Gold Rush was fatal for the Native Americans who had survived Spanish and Mexican rule. This was because white American settlers killed thousands of Native Californians.

The United States had promised to honor property rights of Mexicans in California. But when tens of thousands of Americans swarmed there, U.S. officials took hundreds of ranches away from Mexican residents and gave the land to American settlers.

Chapter Five

The Gold Rush Moves On

When they found gold, Americans ignored the rights of Native people. This 1876 gold mine was in the middle of Sioux homelands in South Dakota.

Moving to Other Areas

By 1854, the California Gold Rush was slowing down. Americans from the East continued to come west, however. Along with forty-niners who never struck it rich, they began **prospecting** elsewhere.

As a result, white Americans began to settle vast areas, such as the Great Plains, which had previously been inhabited only by Native Americans. By the 1880s, the United States basically had achieved its goal to crush all Native groups. Most Natives were confined to reservations, small areas within their homelands. Others were sent from their homelands to reservations elsewhere.

High Expectations

"I confess, without shame, that I expected to find masses of silver lying all about the ground. I expected to see it glittering in the sun on mountain summits. I was perfectly satisfied . . . that I was going to gather up, in a day or two, or at furthest a week or two, silver enough to make me satisfactorily wealthy."

Author Mark Twain, writing about his failed attempt to prospect for silver in Nevada in 1861

THE KLONDIKE NEWS

VOL I.   DAWSON, N.W.T. APRIL 1ST, 1898.   NO. I.

OUTPUT FOR 1898 $40,000,000.

FROM N° 8. EL DORADO.
PROPERTY OF CHAS. LAMB,
VALUE $3,150

DISCOVERER,
GEO. W. CARMACK.

THE LARGEST GOLD NUGGET,

New Strikes

The first big strike after California was in Colorado in 1858, when both gold and silver were found near Pike's Peak. It was the first of many discoveries. Other large strikes were made in Nevada, Arizona, Utah, and Montana.

The Klondike

The last great gold strike was in 1896 in Alaska's Klondike region. The area had been a U.S. territory since March 30, 1867, when the United States purchased it from Russia. Americans had ignored Alaska for years. But when gold was discovered, miners came by the thousands. Despite its harsh climate, Alaska began to develop cities and a small population that would continue growing. Alaska became the nation's forty-ninth state in 1959.

An 1898 issue of the *Klondike News* claims large strikes in Alaska. The Klondike was the site of the last great gold rush.

Conclusion

The Gold Rush greatly speeded up the settlement of California. It also contributed to the rich and mixed culture that is the state's heritage. The gold discovery brought with it an important new influence: today, Asian communities flourish in California and elsewhere in the United States.

California is now known as the "Golden State." It is one of the nation's richest states and has about 35 million residents.

California's state **seal** shows the bear of the Republic and the miner with his pick. The word "*Eureka*" at the top is Greek for "I have found it" and refers to the discovery of gold.

Sutter's Mill Today

California still celebrates the Gold Rush era. People can visit the site of Sutter's Mill and see a full-scale replica of the mill itself in the Marshall Gold Discovery State Historic Park at Coloma. In the early days of the Gold Rush, Coloma was a rowdy mining town with more than six thousand inhabitants and over a dozen hotels. Today, Coloma is a small, quiet community with about two hundred full-time residents.

What Happened to the Mining Camps?

Of the 546 different mining camps started in the Gold Rush, fewer than half survive today. Some, like Coloma, developed into towns. In many cases, however, only their curious names—such as French Corral, Brandy Flat, Scotch Hill, Soggsville, and Rough and Ready—remain as colorful reminders of California's past. Others are still there but as ghost towns.

Ghost Towns

Ghost towns are abandoned communities where buildings still stand, but nobody lives or works in them. During the 1800s, the population of a mining settlement might suddenly grow to several thousand for a few months or years. When the deposits of gold or silver were gone, people would leave as quickly as they had come. All over the West, there are ghost towns from various booms and rushes. Some are ruins, but others have been restored so that people can see what the towns were like during their heyday. Occasionally, ghost towns have a small number of residents, some of them descendants of those who stayed on after everyone else left.

The ghost town of Bodie, California.

Time Line

1769	First of California missions is established.
1821	Republic of Mexico is formed, and Spanish rule of California ends.
1839	Johann Augustus Sutter establishes Sutter's Fort.
1845	United States offers to buy California from Mexico but is refused.
1846	May 13: Mexican War begins.
	June 10: Americans declare an independent Republic of California.
	July 9: United States claims California.
1848	January 24: James W. Marshall discovers gold at Sutter's Mill.
	February 2: Treaty of Guadalupe Hidalgo is signed.
	Mexican War ends.
	California becomes a U.S. territory.
	March 15: The *Californian* publishes the first newspaper story on the discovery of gold.
	August 17: Colonel Richard B. Mason publishes report on the gold strike.
	December 5: President Polk's message to Congress confirms discovery of large amounts of gold.
1849	February 28: First shipload of gold seekers arrives in San Francisco. Ninety thousand people come to California.
1850	California becomes thirty-first state.
1854	Sacramento becomes capital of California.
1856	End of California Gold Rush.
1858	Gold and silver discovered in Colorado near Pike's Peak.
1860	California's population reaches 380,000.
1867	United States purchases Alaska from Russia.
1896	Gold strike in Klondike region of Alaska.
1959	Alaska becomes forty-ninth state.

Things to Think About and Do

Journey to California

In 1849, there were no cars or airplanes, and no trains traveled as far as California. On page 15, read about how the forty-niners traveled to California. Choose a type of transportation mentioned there and find out more about it. Describe a journey in 1849 to California in the West from the United States in the East, using your chosen form of transportation.

Living in Camp

Imagine you are living in a California mining camp. You could be a miner or a cook, a doctor or a musician, a Californian or a foreigner. Write a diary entry describing a typical day in your camp. Describe all the different kinds of people who are there. Tell about the problems and the good things that happen.

Ghost Town

Imagine you are visiting a ghost town built in the days of the Gold Rush. Write a paragraph about some of the things you might find among the ruins that aren't used today. Now pretend you are living in the year 2150 and are visiting a ghost town that hasn't been lived in since the year 2005, or about one hundred fifty years before. Write a paragraph about what you find there, describing everyday things that are no longer used in your time.

Glossary

colony: settlement, area, or country owned or controlled by another nation.

currency: money or anything else used as a unit of exchange in a particular country.

deposit: natural accumulation of a substance, such as gold.

empire: political power that controls large territory usually consisting of colonies or other nations.

expansion: growth in size or area.

fertile: good for growing plants.

immigrant: person who goes to live in a new country or region.

lease: make agreement to use the property of another person.

manifest: obviously true and easily recognizable. When white Americans used the phrase "Manifest Destiny," they meant it was obviously their destiny to take over the American continent.

migration: movement of people or animals from one place to another.

mission: complex built to establish Spanish settlement and exploit the labor of Native Americans living in California.

natural resources: naturally occurring materials—such as wood, oil, and gold—that can be used or sold, or amenities such as a good harbor or climate.

prospect: explore an area looking for mineral resources such as gold or oil.

province: district of a nation that usually has its own capital town and some form of local government, similar to a state in the United States.

republic: nation that has no sovereign or other unelected ruler but is led by a leader or group of officials elected by its citizens.

sawmill: machine for sawing logs.

seal: stamp bearing an official symbol.

shaft: hole going down into the earth at a mining site.

strike: discovery of gold or other precious metal.

treaty: agreement made between two or more people or groups of people.

Further Information

Books

Green, Carl R. *The California Trail to Gold* (In American History). Enslow, 2000.

Ingram, Scott. *California, the Golden State* (World Almanac Library of the States). World Almanac Library, 2002.

Kennedy, Teresa. *California* (From Sea to Shining Sea). Children's Press, 2001.

Press, Petra. *Indians of the Northwest: Traditions, History, Legends, and Life* (The Native Americans). Gareth Stevens, 2001.

Rau, Margaret. *The Wells Fargo Book of the Gold Rush*. Atheneum, 2001.

Web Sites

www.californiahistoricalsociety.org California Historical Society web site has good information about all of California's history, including the Gold Rush.

www.library.ca.gov/goldrush/ California State Library offers excellent online exhibition all about the Gold Rush, including images and original documents.

www.parks.ca.gov/parkindex Index of the California State Park web site will take you to web pages about the Marshall Gold Discovery and Sutter's Fort state historic parks.

Useful Addresses

Marshall Gold Discovery State Historic Park
310 Back Street
Coloma, CA 95613
Telephone: (530) 622-3470

Index

Page numbers in **bold** indicate pictures.